MANAGING
ORGANISATIONAL
· CHANGE ·

A Guide for Managers

Cynthia D Scott and Dennis T Jaffe

KOGAN
PAGE

Copyright © Crisp Publications Inc 1989

First published in the United States of America in 1989
by Crisp Publications Inc, 1200 Hamilton Court, Menlo Park,
California 94025, USA.

This edition first published in Great Britain in 1990
by Kogan Page Ltd, 120 Pentonville Road, London N1 9JN.

Reprinted 1991, 1993, 1994, 1997

British Library Cataloguing in Publication Data
Scott, Cynthia D.
    Managing organisational change.
    1. Organisations. Management
    I. Title   II. Jaffe, Dennis T. (Dennis Theodore), *1946–*
658.4

    ISBN 0-7494-0102-8 pbk

Typeset by the Castlefield Press, Kettering, Northants.
Printed and bound in Great Britain by
Biddles Ltd, Guildford and King's Lynn

Contents

Preface

The present is a time of great entrepreneurial ferment, where old and staid institutions suddenly have to become very limber.

Peter Drucker

Organisational change has become a way of life. Mergers, takeovers, redundancies, deregulation, cutting staff, the introduction of new technology, and increased competition are daily occurrences. As a manager and leader you are under pressure to maintain performance under chaotic conditions. Your workforce may be confused, resistant and disheartened. Job security, company loyalty, and steady career development are no longer available as rewards for performance. What can you do to build a motivated and productive workforce under these conditions?

The skills and strategies outlined in this book will help you to:

- Understand your role in the changing workplace
- Explore what the future workplace will be like
- Lead your team through organisational changes
- Understand and manage people through change
- Provide change leadership
- Use special events to aid transition
- Deal with individual and group resistance
- Negotiate new work arrangements
- Spot common errors
- Prepare your staff for change
- Become a change master

This book will give you the step-by-step advice and activities to become an effective *change leader* in your organisation.

Cynthia D Scott
Dennis T Jaffe

About This Book

Managing Organisational Change is not like most books. It stands out from other books in an important way. It's not a book to read, it's a book to *use*. The unique self-study format of this book and the many worksheets encourage the reader to get involved and try out new ideas immediately.

This book introduces the critical building blocks of how to lead your team successfully through change. Using the simple yet sound techniques presented can considerably improve your ability to help your staff to cope with the traumas of change as positively as possible.

Managing Organisational Change can be used effectively in a number of ways. Here are some possibilities:

- *Individual study*. Because the book has a self-study format, all that is needed is a quiet place, some time and a pencil. By completing the activities and exercises, a reader should receive not only valuable feedback, but also practical steps for self-improvement.

- *Workshops and seminars*. The book is ideal as required reading prior to a workshop or seminar. With the basics in hand, the quality of the participation will improve and more time can be spent on extending and applying the concept during the workshop. The book is also effective when it is distributed at the beginning of a session, and participants work through the contents.

- *Open learning*. Books can be used by those not able to attend in-house office training sessions.

There are several other possibilities depending on the objectives or ideas of the user. One thing is certain, even after it has been read, this book will be looked at – and thought about – again and again.

Introduction

Getting the most from this book

Working with managers and leaders in organisations, the authors have found that the process of organisational change is often alarming and confusing. Yet most organisations have paid little attention to the management of human capital through periods of change. A classic book on mergers and acquisitions devotes only four pages on what to do with the people in the organisation during periods of change. Many companies have discovered that although they have moved the desks, they haven't moved the hearts of the employees who work there. When this happens, management is frustrated by resistance and lack of productivity by the workforce. This book provides the strategies and skills that will help managers through the wilderness of change.

Each change is unique and requires a specialised approach to ensure a positive outcome. There is no single foolproof list of steps to take. Depending on the situation, you as manager must improvise and experiment. We recommend that you use the *Change checklist* in this book as a guide when you undertake a change in your organisation.

Change management is a new skill. None of us studied it as part of our training. In this sense, we are all discoverers and inventors. With the basics of this book and your own common sense and good judgement, you will be able to turn your ideas into positive results when dealing with change.

CHAPTER 1

Understanding Organisational Change

The adaptive corporation needs a new kind of leadership. It needs 'managers of adaptation' equipped with a whole new set of non-linear skills. Above all the adaptive manager today must be . . . willing to think beyond the thinkable – to reconceptualise products, procedures, programmes, and purposes before crisis makes drastic change inescapable.

Warned of impending upheaval, most managers still pursue business as usual. Yet business as usual is dangerous in an environment that has become for all practical purposes, permanently convulsive.

Alvin Toffler, **The Adaptive Corporation**

The pace of organisational change is increasing. Recent studies show that:

- Companies expect to cut an average of 15 per cent of their workforce.
- The hundred biggest mergers in the US during a recent year affected four and a half million workers.
- In the past five years more than 12,000 US companies and corporate divisions have changed hands.
- The take-over trend is increasing. It is more than double what it was three years ago.
- Certain industries have cut a significant percentage of their workforce in recent years.
- British manufacturing needs to increase productivity dramatically to remain competitive with foreign industry.

What changes have you experienced?

Look at the list below and tick off any changes you have faced in the last two years:

☐ technology changes

☐ tighter production schedules

☐ merger

☐ acquisition

☐ divestiture

☐ redundancies

☐ cutting staff

☐ start-up of new division or company

☐ spin-offs

☐ top management change

☐ change of work ethics – new policies, values, expectations

☐ deregulation

☐ reorganisation

☐ serious and new competitors

☐ extra organisational liability

Add your own:

☐ _____

☐ _____

☐ _____

Workplace 2000 – remembering the future

In the past, the definition of management competence rested on specific mangement planning, scheduling, and controlling techniques. Today, competence is based more on attitudes, approaches, philosophies, values and the ability to create improvements in health, innovation, and productivity. A manager today is playing a different game, and must manage in a different way. He or she must be a *change manager*, or, as this book recommends, a *change leader*.

Change leadership is not a skill reserved just for top management. As organisations struggle to respond to the pressures of competition (including the world business environment), you and your work team have to learn to move quickly in order to attain higher standards and increased productivity. Is this possible? In many organisations it is critical; for if you do not succeed, your organisation may not survive.

In recent years, many far-reaching changes have been introduced into the workplace. While the details may vary, change is affecting more and more workplaces and at a faster rate. The reasons are not just 'fashion'. The new strategies are all based on the fact that organisations today need to be organised for constant change. The structures, motivation and pressures within an organisation during change are very different from the traditional processes. Modern organisations ask each individual to take more responsibility and rely more and more on teamwork. The structure of some organisations becomes flatter and less hierarchical.

Looking towards the year 2000

Looking towards the year 2000, the following are some of the elements you can expect to see in most organisations. Tick off any you have already noticed in your own organisation.

I have observed:

☐ more employee involvement in all levels of decision making

☐ increased emphasis on 'meaningful work'

☐ more responsibility for individual employees

☐ fewer managers and more participation in the form of self-managing teams

☐ a move towards profit sharing or employee ownership

☐ an emphasis on human capital as demonstrated by an investment in training, retraining, and new skill development

☐ an atmosphere that encourages more mutual respect and trust

☐ an increase in the protection of employees' rights

☐ workshops that reflect a better attitude by employees towards family commitments

☐ increased encouragement in learning and creativity away from the workplace

☐ better recognition of and reward for superior performance

☐ smaller managerial groups

☐ greater diversity in the workforce with more women and minorities employed

☐ a continuing need for workers with specialised skills

Add others you have noticed:

☐ _____

☐ _____

☐ _____

☐ _____

☐ _____

Learning how to learn

In a constantly changing organisation, no set of skills stays useful for ever. The technical skills a person learns in school, or on the job, quickly become obsolete.

Not long ago a clerical worker had to know how to insert and align carbon paper while typing a document. Today that same person must understand computers, fax machines and, in a larger company, the concept of electronic mail.

Today, it is more important for workers not *to know* a particular set of skills, but to understand *how to learn*. To be successful, people today have to be able to master a wide range of new skills quickly. They have to be open to changing old ways of doing things in order to learn new tasks and adapt to new skills. Most people can't stay in narrow specialisations; they must learn to become more generalised.

What does this mean? First, that every employee will have to take greater responsibility. The authors called this the *two-job concept* in their recent book, *Take This Job and Love It*.* In addition to handling particular job, the 'second job' for an employee is to help his or her organisation to change and improve continuously.

Second, it is no longer possible for a company to guarantee an employee a specific job. If a person wants to remain with an organisation, he or she will have to learn to master many jobs and expect to move around continuously. In many cases, this will be not just in one department or discipline, but broadly, from manufacturing to marketing, or from technical engineering to sales. The most valuable employees will be the ones with the flexibility to master the most challenges.

Third, organisations will have to be recognised into a less hierarchical structure and become more participatory. Teams of workers will be given more authority to decide how to accomplish tasks. Information will have to be widely available, because more groups will need it. As a manager, your role will shift away from the traditional one of controlling and move towards keeping your team trained and flexible in order to accomplish continually changing goals.

Take This Job and Love It, Simon & Schuster, New York, 1988.

Organisational responses to change

Change creates pressure in any organisation. This is especially true when the organisation has not had much experience in dealing with it. The first taste of major change in this situation can be traumatic. Many organisations today are struggling to adjust to the new environment of rapid change.

In many organisations, there are different responses to change among the different level of staff. This is demonstrated below:

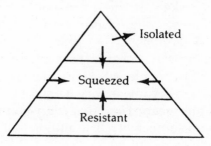

Top management

In a traditional company, top management has a hard time coming to grips with the direct implications of the change. They often underestimate the impact that change has on their employees. They tend to isolate themselves. They often engage in strategic planning sessions and gather information in survey reports. They avoid communicating or seeking bad news, because it is difficult for them to admit they 'don't know'. They expect employees to go along with it when a change is announced and blame their middle managers if people resist or complain about the change. They often feel betrayed when employees don't respond positively.

Middle management

Managers in the middle feel the pressure to make the organisation change according to the wishes of top management. They feel pulled in different directions. Middle managers often lack information and guidance from top management on priorities. They are caught in the middle, and are often confused because they haven't any clear instructions. They feel besieged by upset, resistant or withdrawn employees who no longer respond to previous management approaches, and deserted, blamed or misunderstood by their superiors.

Employees/Workers/Associates

Workers often feel attacked and betrayed by changes announced by management. They are often caught off guard, not really believing that 'my company could do this to me'. Many respond with resistance, anger, frustration and confusion. Their response can solidify into a negative attitude towards the job. They become afraid to take risks, to be innovative or try new things. They experience a loss of traditional relationships, familiar structure, and predicted career advancement patterns.

The role of the manager/leader during change

In times of change each manager, supervisor, and team leader will be called upon to take charge of his or her group. Top management should not be expected to manage the transition of individual work groups. Many middle managers wait for their leaders to tell them what to do. In many cases, communication between top executives and middle managers is poor and there is no effective strategy to announce and implement the change.

Managers want answers. When there are no ready solutions they often blame top management for leaving them in the dark. The best advice for these managers is to stop waiting and become leaders of their team. If they sit around waiting, the wave of change may wash over them and drown them. To stay afloat, they must learn to manage change. Change offers both uncertainty *and* opportunity for them as managers. How they manage themselves and their staff will make all the difference. By following the steps and strategies in this book, they can learn how to view change as an opportunity and create a climate of productivity and growth.

This book was developed to assist you to lead your group in responding effectively to change. Changes can affect your organisational style – the basics of how you do things, your products, customers, management practices, types of leadership etc. Those who know how to react in this environment will be the winners.

Going through any major change will challenge the way we view ourselves. Major changes can be like the death and rebirth of a company. Living through this process is similar to putting in a new kitchen. To obtain the result you want, you first must rip out the old kitchen, leaving only the basic structure and empty space. Then you begin to bring in new units and appliances, which you will fit coherently. Once you add the final touches you can move back in and feel comfortable and productive again. It always takes longer than you thought and costs more than you estimated.

Fantasies about change

Organisational transition is slow, expensive and difficult. There is a tendency to believe that change can be instant, painless, and quick. Managers often seem to expect that changes they make will:

1. Not be disruptive.
2. Not cost too much and be quick to implement.
3. Solve previous organisational problems.

These myths may help you to understand why many organisations do such a poor job of managing the process of change, or become reluctant to accept the challenge of other changes, if previous attempts have gone badly.

The process of making a major change to an organisation's identity requires people to let go of 'how it was' and move through a period of doubt and uncertainty. When you are managing this process it becomes all-consuming and must be done sensitively. Organisations that handle the process of changing a company's identity well reduce the time required for similar changes in the future.

Change of corporate culture

Change is often nothing more than a simple shift in technology, or in the internal hierarchy. But when major change hits a company or a severe crisis demands a response, what is really changing is the 'corporate culture': the way the organisation has been doing things. This amount of change demands a major alteration in the way the work is done. It is no longer possible to remain a caretaker, set in your ways. The new challenge is to increase productivity, while moving your staff in a new direction. This book is about that challenge.

Basic guidelines during change

Here are nine guidelines for changing a corporate, or team, culture. They will be presented more fully in later sections of this book. Whenever possible, you should:

1. Have a good reason for making the change
Substantial changes are not usually much fun. Take them seriously. Make sure you understand why you are making the change and that it is necessary.

2. Involve people in the change
People who are involved are less likely to resist. Being a part of the planning and transition process gives people a sense of control. Ask for opinions about how they would do it. Consider conducting surveys, discussion groups, and opinion polls.

3. Put a respected person in charge of the process
Each change needs a leader. Select someone who is seen in a positive light by your staff.

4. Create transition management teams
You need a cross section of your staff to plan, anticipate, troubleshoot, co-ordinate and direct the efforts towards change.

5. Provide training in new values and work methods

People need guidance in understanding what the 'new way' consists of and why it is more desirable. Training brings groups together. It allows them to express their concerns and reinforce newly learned skills.

6. Bring in outside help

For some reason, there is often more power in what an outsider says than if the same suggestions had come from inside. Use this power to reinforce the direction in which you want to go.

7. Establish symbols of change

Encourage the development of newsletters, new logos or slogans, and/or special events to help celebrate and reflect the change.

8. Acknowledge and reward people

As change begins to work, take time to recognise and recall the achievements of the people who have made it happen. Acknowledge the struggles and sacrifices that people have made.

Review of Chapter 1

You cannot escape or hide from organisational change. It is inevitable. Problems come when people are not allowed to manage the change, and are not taught the skills needed to learn. For an organisation to adapt to change, it must help its workforce to move through change.

CHAPTER 2
Preparing for Change

Key elements of change management
Top management sometimes plans extensively for strategic changes in an organisation, but places very little emphasis on how to handle the transition from the old way to the new. When this happens, the new goal, system, organisation or project is simply presented as a direction or decision to a work team. When the team has not been consulted, this comes as a shock. The change is announced and implementation is left to the group. When this happens to you, as the manager involved, you are put on the spot. You need to produce results but you can only do this when your team is fully behind the changes. Top management too often considers implementation of the change a footnote to their plan. Your work team may consider the same change as a crisis of the first magnitude.

Most of the difficulties manifest themselves in this transition period. This is where people get stuck. They become confused, anxious, angry, and often unproductive. Your job as manager is to move your team through change in the smoothest possible way, regardless of how well or poorly the change was introduced.

Gaining control by giving it up
A major lesson in leadership is that you can't move through change *and* keep previous levels of tight control over your staff. The lesson is to gain control over change by giving it up.

In effective organisations, people share basic goals and

communicate clearly, directly and regularly about what they are doing. Each person goes about his or her work with greater flexibility than is common in less effective organisations. If you manage an effective organisation you will benefit during change by exercising a new type of leadership. You will be less of a controller and more of a coordinator. Only you and your staff together can make things happen. You must learn how to delegate intelligently some of your control to your team.

As manager, you have special responsibilities to maintain strong upward lines of communication. If you keep the information you receive from above to yourself, or feel you are the only one who knows how to handle change, this will not be helpful in implementing the changes. Your staff will not learn, will not have the information they need to make changes and will not feel they share in the change unless you involve them by giving up some of your control.

Power and influence

Most of the major organisational changes you will experience in your career will not be initiated by you. You may be able to anticipate change or see it coming (for example, the need for new technology); however, most of the time change will be handed to you as a fait accompli. When this happens, a typical reaction, regardless of level, is an attitude of helplessness. 'What can I do?' or 'Has anyone taken us into account?' can lead to inactivity and frustration, and workers will spend their time bemoaning the change, dreaming of the old days, or criticising the judgement of top management.

Your task as change agent is to direct energy away from the feelings of powerlessness, and security from the past, and towards seeing the opportunities of the future. You can do this by calling attention to the ways in which your team can make a difference.

Here is how to begin.

Think about a recent change that has been announced in your organisation. Then on the worksheet that follows, fill in which aspects of the change are fundamentals in the space provided. Usually, these are beyond your control. They could include aspects of timing, personnel, budget or any other factors.

Next, write those aspects of the change that you and your team can *control* in the space provided. This is where you need to really think hard. Some things may seem to be fundamental but may in fact be partially under your control.

Finally, think about what aspects of the change you and your team can *influence* and write them down under Negotiable. Remember, you can always communicate or negotiate with other groups in your organisation. Your staff can initiate communication and discussion with any other group. What aspects of the change do you need to talk about, what needs better clarification, and what do you need more information about? How can you accomplish this?

Taking control and exerting influence are crucial aspects of change management. By the end of this book, you will regard almost everything about a change as negotiable. Top management doesn't automatically consider all the aspects. If your team has better information, or sees things differently, you owe it to your organisation to negotiate and discuss it.

Complete the exercise below when you are preparing for a change. Then repeat it with your team to help them plan their response to change. You will find that your team sees things differently from you, just as you often see things differently from your superiors.

Controlling change

Think about a recent change in your organisation and describe which aspect of that change were fundamental, which were negotiable, and which were controllable, in the space provided:

Fundamental – aspects of the change I (we) have no control over:

Negotiable – aspects of the change that we can influence or discuss with other groups:

Controllable – aspects of the change my team can control:

Planning for change

The following steps will help you to introduce and implement a change in your group successfully. You and your team will need to do your homework to complete each stage. Depending on the circumstances, you may not go through each stage in the right order, but you should at least be aware of it. Otherwise you and your group risk not being adequately prepared for implementing the change successfully.

1. **Preparation.** Anticipating key elements of change.

2. **Planning.** Getting people together to plan the response.

3. **Transition structures.** Establishing special ways of working together, and temporary lines of authority.

4. **Implementation.** Putting forward a flexible response, and initiating a training programme.

5. **Reward.** Acknowledging the people who made it work.

Each step will be carefully considered in the following pages. The better you plan, the 'luckier' you will be when implementing change.

Preparation:
Before the change, whenever possible, follow these steps:

1. *Prepare your employees*
   Let them know what is happening in good time. Telling them too far ahead is not always best (for example, telling people eight months before a change leaves too much time for anxiety to build up).

2. *Describe the change as completely as you can*
   How do you see the change affecting individual employees and the workforce as a whole? Identify who will be most affected and approach them first.

3. *Research what happened during the last change*
   Do your staff have a positive history in their ability to manage change, or was the last change traumatic? Learn from past experience and let this influence your current actions.

4. *Assess the organisational readiness of your team*
   Are they ready to undertake a change? An organisation or group that isn't mentally and emotionally prepared will tend to remain in the denial stage, rather than accept the change and move on.

5. *Don't make additional changes that aren't critical*
   People need all the stability they can get during change. Don't change pay days, working hours or canteen procedures when you are making large-scale organisational changes. Change the most important things, one at a time.

Planning
Think it through. During this stage:

1. *Make contingency plans*
   Think of the options the proposed change could bring about. If things go one way, what will you do? What if things go the other way? Anticipate the unforeseen, the unexpected and any setbacks.

2. *Allow for the impact of change on personal performance and productivity*
Don't expect people to adapt immediately to the new work situation. This will frustrate any sense of achievement they may experience.

3. *Encourage employee input*
Discuss each stage of the way and ask for suggestions.

4. *Anticipate the skills and knowledge that will be needed to master the change*
Do your staff possess them? Have you prepared plans for training?

5. *Set a timetable and objectives so that you can measure your progress*

Transition structures
Special activities are required during this special time. After the planning stage, you should:

1. *Create a transition management group to oversee the change*
Develop temporary lines of authority. This group is responsible for taking the pulse of the workforce and helping to identify possible problems.

2. *Develop temporary policies and procedures during the change*
Demonstrate flexibility in trying new things. Loosen control and relax normal procedures.

3. *Create new channels of communication*
Remind people why the change makes sense. Use hot lines, electronic mailboxes, newsletters, videotapes, general meetings, training sessions, posters etc, so that people will receive information fast. The cost of gossip is high: forestall it through clear, accurate communication.

4. *Arrange frequent meetings*
   Meet frequently to monitor the unforeseen, to provide feedback, or to check on what is happening.
   Make feedback a daily event.

Implementation

1. *Provide appropriate training in new skills and develop new attitudes and behaviour patterns*

2. *Encourage self-management*
   Inform each person that he or she is accountable for some aspect of the change.

3. *Provide more feedback than usual to ensure that people always know where they stand.*

4. *Allow for resistance*
   Help people to let go of the 'old'. Be ready to help those who find it particularly difficult to make the adjustment.

5. *Give people a chance to step back and look at what is going on*
   Encourage them to ask 'Is the change working the way we want it to?'

6. *Encourage people to think and act creatively.*

7. *Look for any opportunity created by the change.*

8. *Allow for the withdrawal and return of people who offer temporary resistance*
   Don't dismiss these people as irretrievable.

9. *Collaborate*
   Build bridges between your work team and others.
   Look for opportunities to coordinate your activities.

10. *Monitor the change process*
    Conduct surveys to find out how employees are responding to the change.

Reward

Share out the gains:

1. *Create incentives for special effort*
   Reward those who lead the change. Give one-off bonuses to groups who have come through the change smoothly.

2. *Celebrate*
   Organise special events which publicly acknowledge those groups and individuals who have helped to make things happen.

Review of Chapter 2

You may not know when change is on the way, but when it arrives you will be far from helpless. While much may be beyond your control, many aspects of implementing change can be anticipated and influenced. Begin change management by seeking out new options, and planning. Involve your staff as soon as possible.

CHAPTER 3

What Happens to People?

Understanding loss

Change occurs when one thing ends and something new or different starts. The period between these two points is *transition*. This is where people have to learn to let go of the old and embrace the new. Usually, it means moving from the familiar to the unknown. Even when change is positive, this psychological process affects us. Most of us have a strong response to any change. One of the strongest can be a feeling of loss, along with the struggle to accept a new direction. Change can produce physical symptoms such as sweating, sleep loss, and/or emotional distress which will affect the quality of work.

The most common error in managing change is underestimating the effect it has on people. Many managers think that if they just tell their employees to change, they will. They do not realise how upsetting it is to give up work patterns that are familiar. Always bear in mind the extent of disruption and appreciate that people need time to adjust.

Even when change is positive – promotion, expansion, going public, new markets etc – it is not uncommon to experience a feeling of ending or loss. Managers often have a hard time understanding the loss associated with change. If you don't manage loss, you can't lead people in a new direction.

Types of loss

When a major shift or change occurs within an organisation,

employees normally experience several types of loss including the loss of:

1. *Security*. Employees no longer feel in control or know what the future holds, or where they stand in the organisation.

2. *Competence*. Workers no longer feel they know what to do or how to manage. People sometimes become embarrassed when faced with new tasks because they don't know how to do them. It is hard to admit you don't know how to do something.

3. *Relationships*. Here, the familiar contact with people such as old customers, colleagues or managers can disappear. People often lose their sense of belonging to a team, a group, or an organisation.

4. *Sense of direction*. Employees lose an understanding of where they are going and why they are going there. Meaning and mission often become unclear.

5. *Territory*. There is a feeling of uncertainty about the area that used to 'belong' to them. This can be work space or job responsibilities. Territory includes psychological as well as physical space.

Each of the losses described above has a cost. Any type of loss, even one of work space or familiar technology, can trigger an emotional response that resembles grief. You must help your employees to move past their loss towards acceptance and then to move forward in the new direction.

It is important to understand that people are not weak or old-fashioned if they experience loss caused by change. This is a normal part of transition. In fact, people who do not display any feeling of loss often repress it and can be overcome by a seemingly small transition later on. It is healthier to express and acknowledge loss when it occurs, so that those affected can move through the transition process more quickly. One of the manager's jobs is to acknowledge that a loss has occurred, and not to pretend it is business as usual. Unacknowledged loss will usually lead to resistance and disruption at a later stage.

How people change

People change by being led, not by being told

A common fantasy is that if you order people to change, they will. This belief often leads managers to behave like drill sergeants, ordering employees around. Usually, the response to this approach will be one of resistance, defensiveness and/ or withdrawal.

People do not normally change their behaviour simply by being given information. For example, how many people have given up smoking because of the written warning on a cigarette packet?

It is far more common for people to change because of the *support, encouragement, caring confrontation and empathy* of a relationship. Becoming a leader and being supportive towards your staff is often a new skill for managers, who have hitherto taken a more traditional approach to management. The more involved you are with your team, and the more involved they are with each other, the easier change will be. Creating a trusting relationship requires skill and can put a manager in a more exposed position. However, managers who can create supportive relationships are more successful during periods of change, because their teams will trust and follow them.

Incentives and rewards

Because most change is resisted, it is important to create incentives for those who adapt to change professionally and thoroughly. To become a change agent you might:

- Create public recognition of the change masters
- Reward those who remove obstacles to change
- Give a special one-off bonus to those acquiring the new skills and/or work patterns that make the change successful
- Incorporate good ideas and new suggestions from team members as a regular part of your meetings.

Moving from danger to opportunity

Change often involves elements of both danger and opportunity. When people approach a change, their first response might be to see it as a threat or a danger. When this happens, they fear and resist the change.

Once the change has taken place, it is not unusual for those affected to begin to get used to it. During this period, people often begin to see that the change may lead to new opportunities. Some see that the new way may indeed be more effective and offer the potential for new freedom and power. Once people accept that a change can provide new opportunities and possibilities, the change is well on the way to successful implementation.

Think of a recent change you have experienced and write your reactions in the space provided:

- How was this change experienced by you – as a threat or a danger?

- What hidden opportunities or possibilities did you find in the change?

The transition stages

Danger and *opportunity* can each be further subdivided into the two stages shown below. Altogether, these provide a model of four stages people generally go through when facing change.

- **Danger** can be subdivided into:
  Denial
  and
  Resistance

- **Opportunity** can be subdivided into:
Exploration
and
Commitment

Most people go through these four stages in every transition. However, some may move quickly or get bogged down at different stages. Effective leadership can help a group, and each of its members, to move smoothly through the stages from denial to commitment.

Transition grid

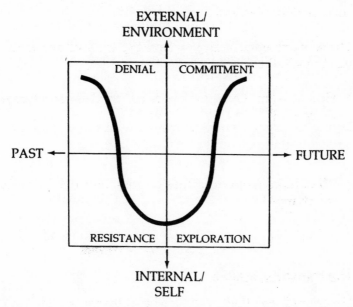

Changes in your organisation will transport your team through the four stages of the transition process shown above. Think of this process as descending into a valley and then climbing back out. The transition leads from the way things were done in the past towards the future. During

The transition grid is part of the Change Programs, Managing the Human Side of Change & Mastering Change, offered by Flora/Elkind Associates in San Francisco and is used with permission.

change, people concentrate on the past, and *deny* the change. Next, they pass through a period of preoccupation, wondering where they stand and how they will be affected. This is normally where *resistance* occurs. As they enter the *exploration* and *commitment* stages, they start to look towards the future and the opportunities it can bring.

Different stages call for different strategies

During change you will probably have employees at different stages. You will need to use your judgement and employ appropriate techniques to help your staff through the change. The checklist below will help you to diagnose which stage employees are at. It is not unusual to find an employee swinging between two stages. In this case, use the strategy described in this section for the earlier stage until that person is ready to move forward.

What do you see in your work group?
During a recent change in your organisation, tick off any behaviour that you have observed within your work unit:

Denial
- ☐ it will soon be over
- ☐ apathy
- ☐ numbness

Commitment
- ☐ teamwork
- ☐ satisfaction
- ☐ clear focus and plan

Resistance
- ☐ can't sleep at night
- ☐ anger/fights
- ☐ 'gave my all and now look what I get'
- ☐ withdrawal from the team

Exploration
- ☐ overpreparation
- ☐ frustration
- ☐ too many new ideas
- ☐ have too much to do
- ☐ can't concentrate

Denial: the first reaction to change

When a big change is announced, the first response is often one of numbness. The announcement doesn't seem to sink in. Nothing happens. People continue to work as usual. It appears as though productivity will continue uninterrupted and nothing will be affected.

The *Denial* stage can be prolonged if employees are not encouraged to register their reactions, or if management expects them to adopt the new ways directly. Denial is harmful because it impedes the natural progression of healing, from loss (ie the old way of doing things) to a movement forward. Employees stay tuned to the way things were (neglecting both themselves and their future), refusing to explore how they can or need to change.

Because people are often blind to problems during the Denial stage, a manager can mistakenly think he or she has jumped directly to the final stage of Commitment. This hope can be reinforced by persuasive speakers who simplistically encourage people to think positively, pull themselves together and move on to excellence. In the USA, this is called a *Tarzan Swing* and it appears to work for a short while (usually until some indicator shows that productivity is decreasing). At this point an organisation may call in a consultant to deal with problems, such as stress, which employees are experiencing. This concentration on the individual, rather than on the organisation's response to the change, leaves an important side of change management untouched.

Top management is particularly prone to want a Tarzan Swing in their organisation from the initial announcement of change. Often they don't see why people should have trouble in adapting. They seem to believe that people are being paid to put aside their feelings, or they may feel that the company simply doesn't have time to move through the other stages. But wishing doesn't change the sequence; it just drives it underground. The next section of this book provides strategies to move a team through the denial stage.

Resistance: the second stage

Resistance occurs when people have moved through the numbness of denial and begin to experience self-doubt, anger, depression, anxiety, frustration, fear or uncertainty because of the change. Some types of organisational change can be likened to a death experience. If a company is sold, merged or suffers redundancies, the expectations, hopes, promises and actual work go through something like a death for certain employees. People concentrate on the impact the change has on them personally.

In the resistance stage, productivity dips drastically and the workforce is often upset and negative. Managers hear a lot of grumbling, the personnel department will be extremely busy and the photocopiers will be churning out CVs. Accidents, sickness and work-related absences multiply. Training programmes on change management are most often requested during the Resistance stage.

While it is difficult for a company to allow negative views to be aired openly, this is exactly what helps to minimise resistance. Allowing people to express their feelings and share their experiences makes this stage pass more quickly. People who believe they are not the only ones who felt a certain way, or think their reactions are more intense than those of their colleagues, feel better when they learn, through open discussion, that others feel the same.

Restrictive organisations which do not encourage responses to be shared, will prolong this stage. Expressing feelings is what helps employees to change. During the resistance period, organisations can make effective use of organisational rituals (eg, parties, awards, luncheons, etc) to encourage people to say what they think. People need a way of saying goodbye to the old and beginning to welcome the new. (Strategies for dealing with resistance will be covered later.)

Eventually, everyone reaches a low point and begins to move up the other side of the change curve. This shift, clearly felt but different for everyone, indicates that things are getting better. Employees suddenly notice a renewed interest in work and feel a return of creativity. This signals that stage two is passing.

Exploration and commitment: the final stages

During the *Exploration* stage, there is an outburst of energy as people turn their attention to the future and towards the external environment once again. This stage could also be described as one of 'chaos'. As people try to fathom new responsibilities, work out new ways of relating to one another, discover more about their future prospects and wonder how the new company organisation will work, many things are called into question. There is a lot of uncertainty during this stage, including stress among those who need a lot of external guidance. During Exploration, people tend to draw on their internal creative energy to work out ways of capitalising on the future. This stage can be exciting and exhilarating. It can create powerful new bonds in a work unit. (Chapter 7 will spend more time discussing planning and exploration.)

After searching, testing, experimenting and exploring, a new form begins to emerge. When this happens, the individual or group is ready for *Commitment*. During this stage employees are ready to commit themselves to a plan. They are willing to redefine their objectives and draw up plans to make them work. They are prepared to learn new ways of working together, and take on renegotiated roles and expectations. The attitudes and work patterns needed for commitment to a new phase of productivity are in place. This is a stage at which employees are willing to identify solidly with a set of goals and be clear about how to reach them. This stage will last until a new cycle of transition begins with another major change.

Since change is inevitable, a good question might be: will we always be riding on this wave of transition? The ideal answer is yes. For without change we and our organisations would become stale and unresponsive. The challenge is in learning to move through the transition as easily and creatively as possible. What helps people to navigate through unknown territory is a map of what they can expect and information as to the most effective ways of responding to the predictable challenges that arise.

Management strategies for each stage

At any given point during the change process, your team is unlikely to be at one stage, but shifting back and forth between stages. As a manager, you need to know what stage your work team is at in general, as well as the one each individual is experiencing. To help your team move through the curve towards commitment, some examples of what you will observe in each stage are listed below. This will help you to diagnose where team members stand.

How to diagnose each phase

Denial
You are likely to see: withdrawal, 'business as usual', attention turned to the past. There is activity, but not much is accomplished.

Resistance
You will see: anger, blame, anxiety, depression, and even a downing of tools: 'What's the difference, this company doesn't care any more'.

Exploration
You will recognise: overpreparation, confusion, chaos, energy, 'Let's try this and this and what about this . . . ?' Lots of energy and new ideas but a lack of coherence.

Commitment
This occurs when employees begin working together. There is cooperation, and better co-ordination: 'How can we work on this?' Those who are committed are looking for the next challenge.

What actions to take

During Denial
Confront individuals with information. Let them know that the change will happen. Explain what to expect and suggest

actions they can take to adjust to the change. Give them time to let things sink in, and then arrange a planning session to talk things over.

During Resistance
Listen, acknowledge feelings, respond empathetically, encourage support. Don't try to talk people out of their feelings, or tell them to change or pull together. If you accept their response, they will continue to tell you how they are feeling. This will help you to respond to some of their concerns.

During Exploration
Concentrate on priorities and provide any necessary training. Follow up projects under way. Set short-term goals. Conduct brainstorming and planning sessions.

During Commitment
Set long-term goals. Concentrate on team building. Create a mission statement. Acknowledge and reward those responding to the change. Look ahead.

Where is your team?
Think about how your work team would respond to change during each stage. Make some notes:

During Denial – I believe my team would react by:

_____

During Resistance – I believe the behaviour of my team would be:

_____

During Exploration – I feel my team would:

_____

During Commitment – My team would probably:

_____

During an actual change

List a few key people in your team and, based on the points already mentioned, make a guess as to where each member is:

Name   **Signs observed**   **Phase**

1. _____

2. _____

3. _____

4. _____

5. _____

Next, draw a graph showing where your members are on the transition grid below. Place their initials approximately where they fall on the curve.

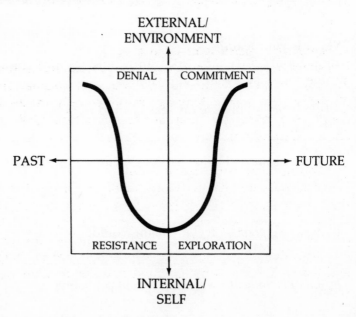

EXTERNAL/
ENVIRONMENT

DENIAL   COMMITMENT

PAST ←   → FUTURE

RESISTANCE   EXPLORATION

INTERNAL/
SELF

Finally, from your analysis, what approaches do you as a manager need to use to bring your team to the next level?

_____

_____

Which are the leaders who can be relied on to help others move along?

_____

_____

Which stragglers in your team need special help?

_____

_____

Traps

During change, a manager may fall into one of the following traps:

1. Ignoring or resisting resistance
Resistance is not pleasant to experience. It can feel as though everyone is angry with you and you are to blame. This is normally temporary. Denying resistance only makes it go deeper and last longer. Invite it. Seek it out through listening and good communication.

2. Forging ahead with team building
When faced with change, many managers think that what they need most is to get people working together again. When a group is in denial, resistance, or the early stages of exploration, it is a waste of time to put too much effort into team building. The group needs a chance to complain and assess their loss before trust and cooperation can be rebuilt.

3. Pushing productivity too soon

Some managers believe that if you demand performance you will get it. Employees may respond in the short term but tend to level out and there may actually be a decrease in productivity if their feelings don't match their actions. The danger is that you will end with a 'clogged' organisation where everything breaks down.

Change mastery

The next four chapters deal with the four competencies that managers need in order to move their teams successfully through change:

Communicating about change
Dealing with resistance
Increasing team involvement
Inspired leadership

CHAPTER 4

Communicating About Change

Communicating with your team

Your role as manager

As a manager, you are often caught in the middle. You may have a lot, some, or virtually no direct involvement in a change, yet you are responsible for making it work in your unit. You will have your own feelings about it. At the same time, you are responsible for taking the company's position.

The way you pass on the message about a change to your team is directly related to the eventual outcome. How you make the announcement, what you say and how you negotiate with your staff can make all the difference. Chapter 4 explores methods of announcing change, explains how to monitor responses and deals with negotiating over what needs to be done. The announcement of change usually comes during the Denial stage, and sometimes it doesn't sink in. When the message is accepted, your team may shift very quickly from Denial to Resistance. You need to learn how to manage these intense responses from your team. This section should help you to do just that.

Setting a climate for communication

In times of change, maintaining open communication can help to prevent rumours, anxiety and mistakes. Managers often avoid delivering unsettling news by claiming they are too busy and under too much pressure to have time to meet the workforce. Studies have shown that if you don't make time early on in the process, you will spend more time later clearing up the problems.

During change, two-way communication is essential. Every issue must be covered. Different communication forms are recommended. Use hotlines, open forums, newsletters, videotapes, friendly chats, informal discussions – whatever works for you. Repeat the message regularly using various methods of communication.

How did I hear?
Let's examine some of the ways in which people learn about change taking your own experience as an example.

Think about a recent change you experienced at work.

- How did you first hear about the change? How were you informed?

_____

_____

_____

- What were the strengths and weaknesses of the way in which you were informed?

_____

_____

_____

- How would you have preferred to be informed? How could the announcement have been improved?

_____

_____

_____

Guidelines for communicating about change

Here are some tips for informing your staff about change. Tick off those you use currently. Put a cross by those you intend to use during the next change.

☐ **1. Address your staff in person**
A memo or newsletter is not the most effective way of informing people about important changes. Written announcements don't allow people to express thier feelings directly. Written documents are often used as a way of avoiding dealing with people's responses. In the long run, this can only be counter-productive. Memos and newsletters are good as a follow-up after a meeting, because people can be in Denial and have a hard time 'hearing' information that disturbs their security.

☐ **2. Tell people the truth**
The more informed people are, the less anxious they will be. Unanswered questions are fuel for gossip-mongers. If you don't know something – tell them. You don't have to know all the answers. A believable leader doesn't know everything, especially in times of change. Encourage questions and try to find answers to the missing information. Arrange another meeting when you have something more to report and share information as it becomes available.

☐ **3. Express your feelings**
Don't exclude information about your feelings. People want to know your reactions. They will feel acknowledged and understood and will be more open if your own feelings are expressed. When appropriate, tell them how the change affects you personally. Self-disclosure from a leader is a very powerful strategy, because you often reflect what your subordinates are thinking.

Here's an example.

'In the light of this new reorganisation, I imagine that some of you are experiencing confusion and anxiety about how this will affect your jobs. As manager of this division I too have some of these worries, but I am confident things will work out for the best. I want to assure you that I will work hard to represent our best interests during the difficult period of transition.

Why is it important to talk?

During times of change, it is important for you to meet your employees both formally and informally. Keeping everyone informed is the overall objective, though the specific purpose of each meeting will vary as you move through the stages of the change process. Here are some specific purposes for meetings:

1. To announce a change.
2. To provide new information and clarification.
3. To give people the right environment to express their feelings.
4. To involve employees in the planning and implementation of the change.
5. To provide feedback on how things are going.

6. _____

7. _____

One interesting observation is that a meeting where change is announced sometimes resembles a miniature version of the four stages of the transition cycle. First, there can be denial until the announcement is discussed and understood. Then people may express resistance by questioning, and complaining or jumping the gun. Next, there can be a shift as people begin to question how they will respond to the future with some constructive brainstorming and planning. Finally, employees may begin tentatively to commit to the direction of the change.

Generally speaking, it's best to call a meeting for the whole workforce if the change affects them all. If some members of staff are more directly affected, you might have individual meetings immediately before the general meeting so that you can explain the situation carefully and/or offer support if appropriate. If individuals are going to be affected negatively, a prior meeting will give you the opportunity to deal with this.

Why do people need discussions?

People who go through change most successfully benefit from:

- Specific reasons for the change
- Accurate information – the truth
- An opportunity and encouragement to ask questions
- Acceptance of the opportunity to express their feelings
- Personal reassurance

Holding a change meeting

A meeting to announce a change is the best way to inform your staff. Meetings are also basic tools for planning, implementing and monitoring change. Meetings reinforce the idea that people are a team which can work together to make things happen. Meetings let everyone know what is happening and offer opportunities for feedback. During change, you should hold frequent meetings to ensure their communication is kept clear and open.

Planning a change meeting

As with any important business activity, it is essential for you to do your homework before conducting a change meeting. Review the information to be communicated. Write notes to ensure all key information is included. Think about the best way of introducing the change and the most logical way of presenting the details. The following is a general format for a change meeting. Make sure you are ready to follow these steps:

- Review the need for change and how it came about.
- Describe the change in detail.
- Explain how the change will affect your staff.
- Ask if there are any questions. Invite participation.
- Listen to people's feelings and respond appropriately.
- Share your personal feelings (if appropriate).
- Ask for help and support in making the change work.

Listening during change

One of the most important elements of communication is listening.* People who feel listened to are less resistant and often adapt to change more easily. 'Active listening' is the best technique for helping individuals to understand their feelings and move more quickly to acceptance.

Listening with the third ear

Some managers frustrate their staff by spending the whole meeting talking. They are so busy announcing, explaining, exhorting and persuading that they don't leave time for questions and answers. Perhaps they are frightened of the reaction. The secret of being a successful change master is not only talking openly and directly, but also listening carefully to what is said – and sometimes what is not said. Listening will help you to understand how your staff feel about the change.

Steps of active listening

During active listening you are paying attention not only to the content of what is being said, but also to the feelings and emotions that lie *behind* it. When you listen actively, you are holding back your need to persuade. That comes later. In active listening, your aim is:

---

* For an excellent book on this topic, read *A Practical Guide to Effective Listening* (Kogan Page)

- to help another person express what he or she feels, and/or wants; and
- to show that you want to understand his or her thinking.

Active listening should include the following points. Tick off those you agree with:

☐ 1. **Pay attention with your whole body**
Sit back and concentrate on the other person. Don't shuffle your papers or fidget. Give him or her your full attention.

☐ 2. **Make eye contact**
Listen with your eyes. Pay attention to what the person says. Observe his or her expression. Try to decipher the body language along with the verbal message.

☐ 3. **Show interest**
Occasionally repeat what the person has just said in order to verify a point (eg 'Let's see, you're saying that the reorganisation will disrupt your career prospects').

☐ 4. **Ask open-ended questions**
Draw the person out. It often takes time to make a point, or reveal honest feelings. Open-ended questions require more than a 'yes' or 'no' answer (eg 'What was your initial reaction to the change?' or 'What do you think the impact of the change will be on the group?').

☐ 5. **Listen to the feelings behind the message**
In addition to what the person is saying, each statement also conveys something about that person's feelings and attitudes. Try to hear not just the content, but the feelings that lie behind it. If you think the person is feeling something, check up by asking a question, such as 'Are you feeling angry about the change?'

☐ **6. Confirm and clarify what you have heard**
Make sure you have understood the message correctly by repeating it back to the person. Try to summarise and get the essence of the person's message across. If you do, the other person will normally be more relaxed and more receptive to discussing options.

Communicating clearly

During change, a manager often assumes that others will understand what to do. Because of increased pressure, there is sometimes a tendency to give fewer instructions and communicate less with your staff. This is a mistake because more information is needed during change, not less. Each staff member needs to assess how he or she will relate to the change. Whether it is a new organisation, a new task, or a new technology, people will need to learn how to work together differently. You will need to bear in mind how relationships within your unit will change, what you expect from each other and how you will work together. Sometimes, you may have to do this several times. During change, things are never static.

Getting your message across

Because communication is the key to change management, it is important for you to communicate fully and clearly.

The following is a four-part formula which will help you to communicate clearly:

> **Situation + Feelings + Effect + Desired outcome =**
> **Clear communication**

Let's look at the parts in more detail:

1. Situation

What has happened? What is the change that needs to be responded to?

> *'Since we started using the new computers, absenteeism has increased significantly. Let's discuss the situation to see if we can discover the reasons.'*

2. Feelings

What are your feelings about the change? Are you confused, hopeful, or upset?

> *'Personally I'm a little frustrated about certain aspects of the change, and would like to know how you feel about it.'*

3. Effect

What effect will the change have on you? The workforce? The project?

> *'The effect of the change has been to put us behind schedule for April.'*

4. Desired outcome

What outcome would you like to see? What do you want the other person to do?

> *'What I'd like is to see if we can work out what is happening and decide what we can do about it.'*

Sending a clear message

Think of a change you're facing. Is there one person you need to inform about any particular difficulty you are having? What message(s) do you need to convey? Write one out below using the formula:

Situation: _____

Feelings: _____

Effect: _____

Desired outcome: _____

Choosing the best words for your feelings

Feelings are hard to communicate because they can be laden with emotion and sometimes indicate an intense reaction. Putting your feelings into words can cause your listener to withdraw, or become defensive. But that doesn't have to happen. Choosing appropriate words can help. It is usually best to select the least dramatic words that still describe the way you feel.

Think of feeling words as falling into three categories:

- 'A' words are very strong. Examples could be: appalled, aghast, disastrous, deceptive, etc. These words should be used with great care.

- 'B' words lie in the medium range. Examples include: concerned, confused, upset, frustrated, etc.

- 'C' words are usually best. Examples are: confused, curious, interested, etc. These are the least likely to evoke a defensive reaction.

People from different cultural backgrounds may put a different interpretation on some words. Make sure you take this into account so you won't startle or offend anyone needlessly.

Feeling Words

A	B	C
____	____	____
____	____	____
____	____	____
____	____	____

CHAPTER 5
Dealing With Resistance

Resistance to change

Identifying signs of resistance

Resistance is not only a predictable part of change, it is perhaps the most difficult phase to deal with. People resist for good reasons, even though we would rather they didn't.

These reasons include the following:

- their security is threatened
- the change threatens their sense of competence
- they fear they will fail at new tasks
- they are comfortable with the status quo.

Signs of individual resistance

How many of these have you observed? Tick them off:

☐ Complaints
☐ Errors
☐ Anger
☐ Stubbornness
☐ Apathy
☐ Absence due to illness
☐ Withdrawal

Signs of resistance can be seen not only in individuals, but also in work units and whole organisations.

Signs of organisational resistance

☐ Accidents
☐ Increased absenteeism
☐ Sabotage
☐ Increase in union activity
☐ Lower productivity

What signs of resistance have you noticed among your staff?

_____

_____

_____

The resistance paradox

Resistance is usually unpleasant for management. It is not easy to put up with complaints or suffer the blame of your employees. Denial seems relatively easier. Sometimes managers encourage their staff to remain in the Denial stage because it is easier for them to manage.

However, resistance is a sign that your group has left the state of denial and is ready to move on. Even though it may be misdirected at first, resistance shows that the person's system of self-defence is beginning to take over; this is an important step in recovering from change.

Your job as a manager is to hold yourself up to exposure and allow yourself (within reason) to receive the slings and arrows of resistance. Remember, you are the firm's representative of the change. Try not to take employee resistance personally.

Rituals: saying goodbye

One of the most successful things a manager can do during change is to help employees to say 'good goodbyes' – so they can say 'good hellos' during Exploration and Commitment. A key element of this process is to accept the discouragement, sadness or grief that employees may be feeling. The intensity of these emotions will vary depending on the intensity of loss they are experiencing. The end of an old system of procedures will be much less emotional than a move to another part of the country.

One way to help your employees through this difficult time is by using ritual. We're not suggesting tribal ceremonies from primitive groups; there are plenty of twentieth-century rituals available. The most successful ones are simple ways of publicly acknowledging the losses that people are experiencing, eg any gathering that brings everyone together to remember the past, tell stories about it and acknowledge how important it was at the time. The next section contains some specific examples.

Examples

- A housing agency, when moving from an old, crumbling building to a new one on the other side of town, cut a piece of the old carpet (a symbol of their past), put it up in their new reception area and covered it with mementoes from the previous location.

- During a merger, employees assembled a time capsule and buried it with old memos, reports etc. As they threw earth on it, they told stories about the past.

Events like these have a way of springing up spontaneously. Management often makes the mistake of thinking such events are childish or unnecessary. When people are not given an opportunity to grieve, they move forward at a slower pace. In the long run, this holds up productivity and prolongs resistance.

Saying goodbye is especially important for people left behind in the case of a reorganisation, merger or buy-out. The 'survivors' often feel guilty, bitter, distrustful and depressed. Those left behind also need a chance to say goodbye to the people who have gone.

Think of a change you are going through. What kind of event could you initiate to help your people say goodbye in a positive way?

_____

_____

_____

_____

_____

_____

Review of Chapter 5

Before people accept a change, they must deal with their feelings about the loss of their old ways. People need time, acceptance and support to let go of the old and move on to the new. The work team can create rituals for saying goodbye, while some employees need special help to move on.

CHAPTER 6
Increasing Team Involvement

Involving your team

The primary complaint of managers during organisational change is the difficulty they experience in getting the workforce motivated. Employees in the early stages of change often seem unmotivated. They are negative, or show no interest in the work that needs to be done. Their attention is elsewhere. The problem is not usually a lack of motivation, but rather that they are dealing with other issues.

Motivation is often thought of as a series of devices managers use to get people to do things. The implication is that without such strategies, employees wouldn't want to do the job.

Newer thinking indicates that people do not have to be tricked into or forced to work. In fact, studies show that most people want to do a good job. A majority of workers responded to a recent survey indicating they are not required to do all that they are capable of in their job. They wished they could contribute even more!

Motivating people is not the same as *making* people do things. It is simply discovering what it is they want to do. People get excited about change when they see a part in it for themselves. They respond with enthusiasm when they feel they have a role in helping to define ways in which the team will be involved in the change. A good leader will offer opportunities for team members to be a part of making change work. This involves asking people for their ideas on how this can best be done.

Role of participation

People will more readily accept change if they are involved in the process. Involvement means that they will have a role in defining how to meet a goal, or respond to a new situation. This is the keynote of participatory management. Participation can take many forms, including:

- Quality circles
- Task forces
- Special discusssion groups
- Question and answer sessions
- Opinion polls
- Suggesion systems
- Brainstorming meetings

As a manager you want to use as many of these methods as possible to involve your employees directly in the change process.

Setting the scene for involvement

Before you begin to involve your employees in the change process, it is important to analyse your motives. Are you involving them because you honestly want to know how they feel, or are you doing it simply to protect yourself from criticism? Many managers have tried involvement and failed because their real intentions were to protect themselves, not to learn.

Test yourself

Which box describes how you really feel?

- ☐ Do you think employees need to be watched closely or they will take advantage of the company?
- ☐ Do you think employees are incapable of suggesting the best way to get something done?
- ☐ Do you make certain your employees check with you every step of the way?
- ☐ Do you manage by staying in your office and issuing commands?

□ Do you personally write up employees' job descriptions etc without consulting them and present them as law?

If you have ticked any of the boxes above, you have a long way to go before you can become a participatory manager, who trusts his employees sufficiently to give them the freedom to define their own ways of working.

Setting goals together

You can help your employees through change by making sure that you involve them in setting the goals for their work. Participative goal and objective setting requires open communication in a problem-solving environment. It is a give-and-take process. A manager who thinks it is his or her sole responsibility to plan, organise, schedule and evaluate work will not be as successful as one who involves employees in goal setting. In times of change, goals and objectives can change frequently and should be re-evaluated often.

Steps for active goal setting during change

1. Assess current situation
2. Listen and repeat
3. Clarify objectives
4. Identify problems
5. Brainstorm for solutions
6. Provide feedback

Let's consider each step individually:

1. Assess current situation – what is happening now?

Does the new work following the change match up to current objectives? How have expectations changed since they were last reviewed? Ask open-ended questions to find out how each employee feels about what is going on regarding new work.

As a manager you may want to become an active listener. Let your employees tell you what is going on. Elicit their ideas on how best to fulfil new responsibilities by asking, *'If you had to do this, how would you go about it?'* or *'If you were the boss and you wanted this to happen, how would you go about it?'*

You can't make improvements unless you know what is going on.

2. Listen and repeat – to establish trust

It is impossible to listen and talk at the same time. Listen for the main idea. Take notes to remind you of what the other person said. Allow enough time for each employee to tell his or her own story completely. Watch out for signs of emotion (what are they feeling/experiencing at this time?). Listen with your whole body. Face the employee with arms and legs uncrossed and lean slightly forward. Establish direct eye contact. Nod your head affirmatively. Say 'Yes' or 'Carry on' occasionally to encourage the employee. Ask open-ended questions (using how, what, where, when, why) and then repeat or re-state what you think the other person said. Ask a question to confirm that you have understood correctly.

3. Clarify objectives – what is it you want and need to achieve?

Work together towards a clear idea of what is wanted. Ask employees to write out their objectives, then meet to discuss and revise them. Working together will give employees the motivation to do well and help to establish a model for performance.

Remember . . . objectives are:

S – specific about what is to be accomplished

M – measurable

A – attainable

R – result or output orientated

T – time limited.

---

4. Identify problems – define and analyse the problems

When setting goals, there will be some areas in which you and your employees might not agree. During periods of change it is usual either to have too many objectives (the result of combining jobs without narrowing down objectives) or to produce work that fits both the old and new ways of doing things. As a manager, your job is to help to put objectives in order of priority to avoid a situation where the employee is overwhelmed. Too many objectives will create anxiety and lead to poor performance.

5. Brainstorm for solutions

During change it's usual for jobs to change character. Previous job descriptions are often no longer applicable and employees may feel upset if they are being asked to do things that are 'not part of their job'. To help employees understand their new roles, you need to consider:

What has been tried before?

What have other people done in similar situations?

What have you tried before, which may not have worked then but might work now?

6. Provide feedback

Feedback is essential to employees during change. They need to know how they are getting on. They need encouragement and support. Many managers don't do a good job of providing feedback when things are normal.

Tick any reasons you have used for not providing feedback and then resolve to change your ways:

☐ They already know what I think.

☐ I'm the boss, so they have to follow my instructions.

☐ I have too many other things to do.

☐ If there's anything new, I'll tell the people who need to know.

☐ They're professionals – they shouldn't need their hands held.

☐ _____

When feedback is poor, employees are more likely to be anxious, experience low job satisfaction, or give notice. People who hear nothing usually fear the worst.

How to improve your feedback

The purpose of feedback is to help your employees to change their work methods in a way that improves their performance. Provide feedback either in the form of information or as a course of action. When you provide 'action-oriented' feedback, make sure it is something your staff can control. You will only create frustration if you ask them to tackle something that is beyond their control. Here are some tips:

1. Be direct

Give feedback in person. The more people a message goes through, the more likely it is to be distorted. Also, give it as soon as you can.

2. Be specific

People learn from complete information. What jobs, work patterns etc do you want them to continue or discontinue? Simply saying *'Good job'* doesn't provide much information. It would be much better to say: *'Thank you for staying late last night to get that shipment out to Mr Allen. I really appreciate your giving up your own time.'*

3. Be personal
Add something of yourself to the feedback. Make it sound personal by expressing your feelings, eg *'I am rather concerned about your work performance'* or *'I was very proud when you were nominated for the safety award.'* This makes feedback more meaningful. Employees want to hear from *you*.

4. Be honest
Employees can tell when you are insincere. If the feedback isn't genuine, don't give it at all.

Reward attempts, not just achievements
Mistakes will be made during changes. How you react to them is important if you wish to maintain employee involvement. Each mistake represents a potential for learning. It is your job to point out to employees the learning aspect of the mistake. Ask what they will do next time to prevent the mistake from happening again. Back them up in their ideas and give them your support when they try again.

One way to reduce the damage from mistakes is to have regular reporting and feedback sessions. This is especially important during changes when the former ways of working are often no longer applicable.

How performance is affected through change
Change in the workplace will affect your employee's job performance. Performance will usually be affected in direct proportion to the magnitude of the change. If the change is significant it is safe to assume that work activities will not be accomplished at a normal rate. Allow for this in your production planning and scheduling.

Before, during and after change, employees want specific things from their jobs. Make sure you provide as many of the following as possible:

1. Work that is interesting and/or meaningful.
2. A clear statement of the results you expect.
3. Appropriate and immediate feedback regarding those results.
4. A system of rewards for results achieved.

Change provides you with an excellent opportunity for re-thinking job descriptions and assignments and making them more meaningful. Job enrichment can be nothing more than redefining a current job by involving the employee in such a way that it becomes more fulfilling. This may involve adding responsibilities, varying or rotating tasks, or finding new ways of doing the job.

Describe a job in your area that may be a candidate for enrichment.

_____

_____

Redefining a job

Use the following steps to job enrichment in redefining jobs during change. Analyse how a job is done at present.

1. Procedures

_____

_____

_____

2. Tools/Techniques/Skills required

_____

_____

_____

3. Scope of authority. Who supervises? What is their authority?

_____

_____

_____

4. Schedule for completing work

_____

_____

_____

5. Internal relationship – who does the employee work closely with?

_____

_____

_____

6. Anything else that is essential

_____

_____

_____

Look at the information you assembled above and rethink each job using the following principles:

1. What is the overall objective/direction/meaning of the job? Is the job a coherent whole rather than a number of disjointed parts?

_____

_____

_____

_____

_____

2. How can you get across to the employee that the job makes a contribution? What are the limits of individual accountability?

_____

_____

_____

_____

_____

3. How can the employee participate in the planning process?

_____

_____

_____

_____

_____

CHAPTER 7
Inspired Leadership

Being a leader during change

Being a leader during a period of change is not easy. Different management skills are needed. There is less hands-on control and more liaising and co-ordinating. The sphere of control is often increased and managers may be responsible for more people and different challenges. To succeed, an active leader will do more to direct the efforts of his or her employees. This requires:

- Having and articulating an overall view of where the group is going
- Sharing that insight
- Creating an environment in which employees wish to participate in this view of the future.

Many managers say they feel powerless to manage during change, as they are squeezed by pressures from above and below. In this section you will acquire what tools you can use to lead your team into the future. They do not require top management's approval to implement; remember what was said earlier – if you are waiting for your company to tell you how to change before you can lead your team forward, you may be waiting a very long time.

Step 1
Creating a view of the future
When change occurs, we have to move from 'how it was' to a

vision of 'how it will be'. After a group has progressed beyond Denial and Resistance, it is usual to experience an upsurge of energy. People start getting ready to face the future. They start to explore where they stand, what new results need to be achieved, and what opportunities lie ahead. At this stage, they need help to create a view of their goal. This is where you can help to lead your team towards a shared vision of the future. Many of the extraordinary things achieved by ordinary people begin with a vision that inspires and empowers them. During a time of transition, a change leader will help his or her group to establish a clear set of directions to be followed.

Step 2
Looking into the future
Set aside some time to discuss the future. Arrange a special meeting to concentrate on looking ahead.

Ask your team to close their eyes and imagine themselves in five years' time. The major upheaval is over and everything has settled down again. Ask your staff what they notice about their workplace of the future. How is it organised? What are people doing? What are the work areas like? What type of work is being done? As they explore this workplace of the future, ask them to think about how the future differs from today. What improvements do they see?

Next, hold a discussion on how people saw the future. Write down the key points on a flip-chart. Create a shared vision of the future.

OUR VISION OF THE FUTURE IS:

This type of planning can be an exciting process. It can help employees to realise that they play a part in shaping their future. Instead of worrying about an uncertain future, looking ahead together can help a team to generate a shared sense of direction. It is possible to work backwards and design ways of reaching this vision.

Step 3
Clarifying values
Change can lead to a reappraisal of the values your team operates by. Values are the foundation of the way you work together. During change, basic values may shift. For example, a company that once valued strict procedures and tradition may change by placing more emphasis on independence and new markets. You may find it useful to clarify what the former values were and what the new values will be.

Work values exercise

A *value* is a principle or standard that you consider worthwhile and that you use to live or work by. The following values are common in a work environment. How important is each member of your team? Make a copy of this form and ask each member of your staff to complete the exercise individually.

	Least important		Most important		
Security – freedom from worry, safety, certainty, predictability	1	2	3	4	5
Status – how you appear in the eyes of others	1	2	3	4	5
Pay or remuneration	1	2	3	4	5
Advancement – improvement, progress	1	2	3	4	5
Affiliation – being associated with and liked by colleagues	1	2	3	4	5
Recognition – being noticed for individual or team effort	1	2	3	4	5

	Least important				Most important
Recognition – being noticed for individual or team effort	1	2	3	4	5
Authority – having the power to direct events	1	2	3	4	5
Achievement – mastery of task, project or skills to get job done	1	2	3	4	5
Independence – freedom from control of others	1	2	3	4	5
Altruism – concern for the well-being of others	1	2	3	4	5
Creativity – finding new ways of doing things, being innovative	1	2	3	4	5
Intellectual stimulation – critical thinking, new ideas	1	2	3	4	5
Aesthetics – desire for beauty in work and surroundings	1	2	3	4	5
Other values important to your group					
_____	1	2	3	4	5
_____	1	2	3	4	5
_____	1	2	3	4	5

After each team member has clarified his or her personal values, lead them in a discussion about the group's shared values and try to come up with the main work values suggested by your team.

The main values of our team include:

_____

_____

_____

Keep the discussion of values concrete. Don't let people talk in abstractions. Give specific examples of what acting according to these values might consist of.

For instance, an example of commitment could be finding someone to stand in for you when you have to take time off from work.

Don't be afraid to talk openly about values that may be obscured or forgotten due to business pressures.

Values are the new gel
Shared values allow you to work together using a balance of delegation and control. During a time of change, you will probably find your sphere is growing to include a wider range of values. This is normal. Traditional work ethics were often narrowly defined and demanded a high degree of conformity. There was a 'right' way of doing things and if you wanted to belong, that was the way you did them. Today, with traditional standards in flux, there is a wider range of what is 'right', and more room for creativity, individual initiative and change. The new work team operates not according to tradition, but using vision and shared values. Team members in the future will have to make more independent decisions. Your job as a team leader is to keep them enthusiastic and committed to the targets they have set.

Finding the new way
After a team has clarified its vision and values, your task as a change leader is to help your staff to explore how they can best accomplish their goals. It will then be possible to draw up and adhere to a plan of action.

Drawing up a plan of action

An action plan can arise out of a brainstorming meeting, or series of meetings, where employees feel confident about suggesting ideas of how to accomplish goals based on the group's shared vision. Sometimes, when new technology is brought in or a significantly different organisation initiated, many changes may be required as a result.

Exploration is the period of time when your team makes an extra effort to think about new ways of doing things. A team, when working well, can often think of more and better ways of achieving results. Draw on the energy of the team to think about how to make positive things happen.

Planning sessions may seem inefficient. But you will find planning well worth the time. People want to participate and become involved. They will often spend their own time resolving specific challenges.

After a period of brainstorming, you should lead your group on to making some decisions. This means setting specific goals and agreeing on a plan to meet them. Making decisions as a team helps everyone's commitment to them.

Once you are committed to new goals, you should take the time to recognise the contribution each individual has made.

CHAPTER 8

An Action Plan for Success

It's now time to put together all you have learned, and create an *Action Plan* for responding to change in your workplace. Answer each of the questions below for changes that you face:

1. Describe the change as completely as you can. State specifically how it will affect your employees, department and organisation. Note 'human factors' that will be affected by the change.

   _____

   _____

   _____

   _____

2. How do you imagine the best possible outcome?

   _____

   _____

   _____

   _____

3. What are the strengths of your group/department in undertaking this change?

   _____

   _____

   _____

   _____

4. What obstacles will the change bring to prevent you from reaching your goal?

_____

_____

_____

_____

5. List the action steps for:

Communication _____

_____

_____

Dealing with resistance _____

_____

_____

Involvement _____

_____

_____

Leadership _____

_____

_____

_____

6. What is your timetable for making this change?

Start _____

_____

_____

_____ Finish

7. What new skills, knowledge and attitudes are needed to make this change?

Skills _____

_____.

_____

Knowledge _____

_____

_____

Attitudes _____

_____

_____

8. *How will you acknowledge, recognise and celebrate this change?*

_____

_____

_____

_____

9. *How will you create incentives to move toward change?*

_____

_____

_____

_____

10. *How will you reward yourself for having led this change?*

_____

_____

_____

_____

Further Reading

Bennis, Warren and Nanus, Bert. *Leaders*. Harper and Row, 1985.

Deal, Terrence, and Kennedy, Allen A. *Corporate Cultures*. Penguin, 1984.

Hirschhorn, Larry and Associates. *Cutting Back*. Jossey-Bass, 1983.

Kanter, Rosabeth Moss. *The Change Masters*. Allen & Unwin, 1984.

Kilmann, Ralph. *Beyond the Quick Fix*. Jossey-Bass, 1984.

Miller, William. *The Creative Edge*. Addison-Wesley, 1987.

Morgan, Gareth. *Riding the Waves of Change*. Jossey-Bass, 1988.

Peters, Tom. *Thriving on Chaos*. Macmillan, 1988.

Pinchot, Gifford. *Intrapreneuring*. Harper and Row, 1985.

Tichy, Noel and Devanna, Mary Ann. *The Transformational Leader*. John Wiley, 1986.

Torbert, William. *Managing the Corporate Dream*. Dow Jones Irwin, 1986.

Woodward, Harry and Buchholz, Steve. *Helping People Through Corporate Change*. John Wiley, 1987.

Books from Kogan Page

Don't Do. Delegate! The Secret Power of Successful Managers, James M Jenks and John M Kelly, 1986

The First Time Manager, 2nd edition, M J Morris, 1994

How to Be an Even Better Manager, 4th edition, Michael Armstrong, 1994

Quality at Work, Diane Bone and Rick Griggs, 1989

Better Management Skills

This highly popular range of inexpensive paperbacks covers all areas of basic management. Practical, easy to read and instantly accessible, these guides will help managers to improve their business or communication skills. Those marked * are available on audio cassette.

The books in this series can be tailored to specific company requirements. For further details, please contact the publisher, Kogan Page, telephone 0171 278 0433, fax 0171 837 6348.

Be a Successful Supervisor
Be Positive
Building High Performance Teams
Business Creativity
Business Ethics
Business Etiquette
Coaching Your Employees
Conducting Effective Interviews
Consult Your Customers
Counselling Your Staff
Creating a Learning Organisation
Creative Decision-making
Delegating for Results
Develop Your Assertiveness
Effective Employee Participation
Effective Meeting Skills
Effective Networking
Effective Performance Appraisals*
Effective Presentation Skills
Empowering People
Empowerment
Facilitation Skills for Team
  Development
First Time Supervisor
Get Organised!
Goals and Goal Setting
How to Communicate Effectively*
How to Develop a Positive Attitude*
How to Develop Assertiveness
How to Improve Performance
  through Benchmarking
How to Manage Organisational
  Change

How to Motivate People*
How to Plan Your Competitive
  Strategy
How to Understand Financial
  Statements
How to Write a Marketing Plan
How to Write a Staff Manual
Improving Employee Performance
Make Every Minute Count*
Making TQM Work
Managing Cultural Diversity at
  Work
Managing Part-Time Employees
Marketing for Success
Memory Skills in Business
Mentoring
Negotiating Skills for Business
NLP for Business Success
Office Management
Personnel Testing
Process Improvement
Productive Planning
Project Management
Prospecting
Quality Customer Service
Rate Your Skills as a Manager
Successful Presentation Skills
Successful Telephone Techniques
Systematic Problem-solving and
  Decision-making
Team Building
Training Methods that Work
The Woman Manager